Letters to a Shooter

Letters to a Shooter

by
Oscar Valdes

This book is a production of Editorial Madruga,
P.O. Box 78, Pasadena, CA 91102

You may visit the author online at oscarvaldes.net.

Library of Congress Control Number: 2018908388

Published 2018
Printed in the United States of America
Print ISBN: 978-0-9793558-9-9

Cover and interior design by Ann Valdés

For my daughter
&
for Teresa, Jody, Ray, Tona, Isabela and Victoria.

With every breath you take in, say
I am a man,
I am a man with murderous thoughts,
I am a man,

Hold the breath and let it out slowly,
and repeat
I am a man,
I am a man with murderous thoughts,
I am a man,

Keep breathing – in and out - while saying to yourself,
I am a man with murderous thoughts
who's on the verge of hurting others
who have been through the same pain
I am now having,

I am a man

Keep breathing, please

I am a man

In pain

$\mathcal{S}$o you're thinking of loading up and stepping into
a crowded place and letting them have it.
It could be a school, a concert, a church, a busy street.
Your pain – because it has to be pain that's pushing you to
even think about it – is causing you to come up with a plan to
hurt and kill other people.
People like you and me.
People you have met and not met.
People you have a grudge against and people you don't have
a grudge against.

Wow.

Brother, that has to be a lot of pain you're carrying.
A lot.
So much so that it is crushing you.
So much so that it is taking your life out of you.

Your life.

Maybe you're already thinking of what the newspapers will
say.
"Shooter in Anytown kills x number of folks"
and then your photo up there, along with the news of the
day,
news about what the President said or how the economy is
doing.
Your moment in the sun.
You up there, with the big boys and the big girls.

I wish someone would be there right now. Next to you.
Anyone.

Another person who would be a witness to your pain.
Who would listen to you and say,
that's a lot of pain you're carrying,
so much so that it's deadened you inside.

I wish someone would be there right now,
next to you,
who wouldn't compare you with anyone else,
but see just you.
Someone
who would give you their complete attention.

I wish someone could be there right now,
next to you,
so you would tell them just how deep your pain goes
and how you've never shared it,
never let another person hear you out.

Just hear you out.

We're not made to carry a lot of pain.
Nature didn't design us that way.
We can carry some but now and then we have to look at it,
break it down,
stare at it,
make sense of it,
so that it can become bearable.
Otherwise it rots something inside of us,
smudges our windows to the world
and we don't see clearly.
Pain does that.

Everyone has pain.
Everyone.
Even those who look like they have it all.
Like a movie star.
He, or she, has pain too.

I have never met you but I know something about you.
I know you feel very alone.
Even though I've never seen you.
I know that.
And I know that you think you can't handle your pain.

But you can learn.

$\mathcal{B}$reathe,
In and out
slowly
and say,
I am a man with murderous thoughts
I am a man,
I am a man in pain
I am a man,
I am a man in pain with murderous thoughts.

Breathe,
In and out,
slowly
and say
I am a man in pain and I can live with it
I am a man,
I can live with the pain
yes I can,
I can live with it.
The pain will not kill me,
no, I won't let it
I am a man

Breathe,
in and out
slowly
I am a man in pain and I can hold it
yes I can,
I can hold my pain
and will not give it to anyone else,
I am a man in pain and I can hold it

I am a man,

I am a man in pain who can talk about it
yes I can,
and will not give my pain to anyone else
I am a man,
I will not hurt others
I am a man.

●

$\mathcal{U}$p until the moment you pull the trigger you've
got a chance
no matter how flawed you think you are,
you still have a chance

But after you pull the trigger it's all over.
You've crossed the line.

You've got to stay on this side,
the side of your pain,
the side of not squeezing the trigger,
the side of your feelings and your thoughts.

And to own them,
to accept them.

Now say with me,
these are my feelings,
these are my thoughts,
no matter how bizarre they may be.

And I want to share them with another person.

Let's say it together,
these are my feelings and thoughts
and I want to share them with another person.

Don't think you need another person?
That's the beginning of the road to trouble.
Being human means a lot of things
but one of them is that we need others.
From the get go.

From the moment we're conceived.
Without others we don't get to first base,
we don't even get to hold the bat.

*W*e're all flawed.
And that means this person who wrote these words.

I wrote them for you.

I've never seen you, never heard of you,
but I know I have something in common with you.
I am flawed.
And so is every human being.
Without exception.

But if you're thinking of pulling the trigger
and killing others,
then you have a lot more pain than I do.
A whole lot more,
and I am sorry about that.

No one should have so much pain.

I am here to tell you that you can work with it.
No matter how unbearable it may seem,
you can work with it.

But if you kill another person then you're killing yourself.
Even if you survive the incident and don't commit suicide
after the fact.

If you kill another person you're not only putting an end to
whomever that person is
and could become,
you're putting an end to your possibilities, too.

The headlines for that day or for that week,

during your trial and sentencing
if it goes that far,
add nothing to your life.
All they say is that you could not handle your pain,
that you did not square with yourself and accepted
what you were going through,
that you gave up and chose to give it to others instead.

There is no glory in that.
No glory in taking other people's lives
because you couldn't handle your pain.

Pulling the trigger on innocent people
does not make you a hero.

They did nothing to you.
Never harmed you.
Don't even know you exist.

$\mathcal{D}$o you want to be a hero?

If you extend yourself for other people,
make an effort to help those in need
or put your life at risk to save others,
you may become one.

There are many instances of heroism,
small and large,
every day in our world.
Most we don't hear about.

You could be a hero if you wanted to.

So say with me now,
I am a man,
I am a man in pain,

Breathe in and out,
slowly,
and say with me,
I am a man in pain thinking murderous thoughts,
wanting the world's attention
and willing to sacrifice others
to have that attention,
if only briefly.

But it doesn't make any sense.

Sacrificing people,
killing or injuring others because you have pain
that you're unable to understand and transform

is a form of insanity. A form of madness.

Emotions that are not understood and processed
can make us insane.
It doesn't matter how rational you may be
in putting together your plan to hurt others.
If you are targeting innocent people
then you are mad.
Mad as in insane.

But you can defeat your madness
if you share your pain.

Again,
Breathe in and breathe out,
slowly
and say with me,
I will defeat my madness
yes I will,
I will defeat it,
yes I will
because I can,
and I will defeat it
when I share my pain with another human being.
I will defeat my madness
when I talk about my pain with another human being.

Breathe in and breathe out.

I will defeat my madness
when I talk about my pain with another human being.

•

*N*ow imagine for a moment
what it would be like to be in the living room
of parents who have just learned that their son or daughter
had been killed by you.

Imagine for a moment. Please.

Just imagine.
Imagine the love they gave to their son or daughter,
all the sacrifices they made to do well by
the person they had brought into this world,

Just imagine
the depth of the pain they're feeling.
The agony.

I can only imagine.

Can you?

Please try.

Because that's on you if you pull the trigger.

Can you not feel your pain?
Can you not see it?
Do you have to give it to another person to feel it?
Do you have to give it to another person to see it?
Are you numb and blind to it?
Can you not see what you're about to do?
To yourself and to others?

Breathe,
please,
slowly, in and out
and say with me,
I will not give my pain to others.

Instead, I will talk about it.
Instead, I will share it.
Instead, I will reach out.

Yes.
There is kindness in the world.
Reach out and it will come.

Breathe,
in and out,
and say
I am a man,
I need to understand my emotions,
if I don't, then they will rule me,
if I don't, then I will be at their mercy,
if I don't, then I will not be in charge of my life.

Breathe,

I am a man.

If I were beside you I would put my hand on your
shoulder
and tell you that
no matter how unbearable your pain seems,
there is a way to lessen it,
to ease it,
and the first step is to share it,
the second to understand it,
the third to transform it.

And if you take the first step
you're on the way to the second
and then to the third.

And it starts with you picking up that phone
and reaching out to another human being.
Someone who can come to your side
and put their hand on your shoulder
and look you in the eye.

And you will know you're not alone.

It's difficult to be alone sometimes.

Very difficult.

But the moment you say that first word,
just that one word,
the moment it sails out of you and reaches the other person,
then you know you're not alone.

It's horrible to be alone and in pain,

and it may seem like a labyrinth with no way out
but there is a way,
and if you take that first step,
if you say I am human and I need others,
then the path lights up right in front of you.

And you will be stronger
and you will be wiser,
and live to see what your efforts can make happen.

I am a man.

*I*f you're thinking of pulling the trigger and killing
innocent people
then there's no love in your life.

I know that even if we have never met.

If you're thinking of killing innocent people
then you do not know what love is.
You have never had it in your life.

You may have felt attracted to someone
and thought it was love.
You may have desperately needed someone
and thought it was love.
But if you're thinking of hurting innocent people
you do not know what love is.

It's pretty sad to go through life without knowing what love
is.

Darned sad.

When you truly love,
even if only once in your life,
there's a freedom that comes to you.

When you truly love and the loved one walks away from you
you may be angry
but you do not wish them harm.

Instead you grieve your loss and say to yourself,
with that person I felt love,

and sadness and pain,
and that love made me see life differently,
and I am grateful to that person for helping me get there.

Having felt true love makes you smarter,
in countless ways,
Makes you deeper
in countless ways,
and you become a better human being.

Do you want to learn how to love?

You can.

There's a certain sadness in love
because the person you love cannot be everything you want
them to be.
And that's okay.
Remember,
we're all flawed.
Incomplete.

Your loved one is flawed, too.

But there's an energy that comes from the bond of love,
an energy that moves you up a peg or two
in your personal confidence,
a peg or two
in your feeling more grounded.
Accepted.
Valued.
And as you do for your loved one

you will feel enriched,
because in the giving you enlarge yourself,
and so too your capacity to view the world around you.
But how do you start?

You listen to your heart.

That's it.
And if you feel a tug
you go with it.

Hi, you say.
And you smile.

Your heart will show you the rest.

So take the chance.
And if you flop, you flop.
Or as a friend of mine once told me,
they weren't meant for you.

Can't take the risk?
Yes, you can.
Do you not love yourself a little?
Yes, you do.
Enough to take that first step.

So own it.
And try again.
And again.

We cannot stop loving.

If you're knocked down
you get up and try once more,
never giving up.
We all have to do that.
It's being a human being 101.

*W*hen I was twenty I had a friend who committed
suicide.
Romulo was his name. After the mythical founders of Rome.
Romulo was a poet.
He had written beautiful poems to the woman he adored
but she did not love him.

I had not seen him for a good while
when I heard the news.
After the initial shock I got angry.
Why had he not reached out to any of his friends
who so esteemed him?
And I grieved for him
and for all that he could have contributed to the world.

I never met his beloved
but I am sure that she, too,
if she dared to love,
would one day not have her love returned.

It happens to every single one of us.
No exceptions.

But my dear friend Romulo
could not handle the pain
and it had crushed him.
Master of words that he was,
he had failed to see his way out of his labyrinth.

The loss. The pain.

If you pull the trigger,

how many lives will that cost us,
including yours?

You don't know, trapped as you are,
all that you may contribute during your lifetime.
You don't know
what you may give to the world,
if you learn to handle your pain.

I am a man.

*S*ay with me, this is my life.
Repeat,
this is my life.
Mine.

It is miserable. Horrible.
Repeat,
it is miserable, horrible.

If you need to shout it out do so.
This is the moment.
Stand up and bellow it out.
No matter what time it is
or if you wake up the neighbors,
just put it out there.
Let the world listen,
let the rest of us hear it.

If there's no one around to hear you
then use your imagination and put someone you value right
in front of you.
Look them in the eye.
Please.
Look them in the eye and
say to them,
I am in pain,
my life is miserable, horrible.

Again,
Look them the eye,
please,
and say to them,

I am in pain,
my life is miserable, horrible.
But it can be better. It will get better.
Did you hear me?
I just said that. I just sent you that thought,
that wish of mine,
that wish of mankind,
of your brothers and sisters the world over.

So please say
I will share my pain,
I will scream it out if I need to,
and even though no one may come to my side right away
if I keep saying it, someone will.

So say,
I will not give my pain to others but will share it instead.
I will be sharing my pain
when I speak or shout it out.

That is your responsibility,
to not give up,
but to fight.
Because you have a mind.

The moment we have a mind we acquire the obligation to be
responsible
to ourselves and to others.

Those who don't have a mind need to be cared for.

The rest of us,

those of us who do not have at this moment
the same pain that you have now,
have an obligation as well,
an obligation to hear you,
to listen carefully to what you have to say,
an obligation to hear your pain,
yes,
hear it,
and together restore in you
the will to fight.

Pulling the trigger and killing others
is not fighting the fight.
It is giving up.

Pulling the trigger and killing others
is taking to the grave innocent people,
people who have much to give us all,
including to you.

Please say,
I am a man.
I will not give my pain to others but share it instead.
I will share my pain so I can understand
and transform it.
I am a man.

*M*ost of us men have known cowardice at some
point in our lives,
cowardice,
disgraceful fear or timidity says the dictionary,
cowardice,
the inability to assert oneself physically, emotionally, or
intellectually,
say I.

But if the fears that block us are understood,
if they are examined,
then they can be conquered.

Overcoming cowardice is a life long struggle.

We are all different,
and so, too, our gifts and abilities,
and it is each person's responsibility
to create his own space in this world,
and it will not happen unless
you put effort into it.

I have a right to be here,
all of us must say,
a right to my body, no matter what size, color or shape,
a right to my emotions, no matter how varied or jumbled,
a right to my thoughts, no matter how unformed or unclear.

That's where we start,
and because the effort may take a lifetime,
it is no surprise that, being different,
at any given point

we find ourselves at various levels of development.

Pulling the trigger and killing innocent people
is not asserting yourself physically, emotionally or
intellectually.
Pulling the trigger and killing innocent people
is bailing out,
giving up on the task of your growth as a person
and as a man.

Pulling the trigger and killing innocent people,
no matter how big your guns and how elaborate your
reasons,
is an act of cowardly cruelty.

We are all capable of it.
All of us.
But thankfully,
most of us choose the task
of creating our own space.
Most of us choose the task
of discovering what gifts we have.

And it takes a lifetime.

We discover our gifts as we overcome our cowardice.

Now
say with me again,
I am a man,
I will not give my pain to others,
I will face and conquer my cowardice

like all of us must,

you and me,

all of us,

I am a man.

•

A few years ago
I had to have surgery in my belly.
I had a tumor growing inside.
After the operation I was given medication for pain but it
made me sick
so I chose to stop it.

I felt alone and anxious.
My life hadn't been going the way I wanted.

Then there came a moment,
as I lay in the hospital bed
surrounded by tubes and drips and monitoring machines,
that I thought I was not going to make it out.

I called for help.
The doctors came and I told them,
I do not think I am going to make it out.

They listened.
They would give me something to calm my anxiety
they said,
but please take the medicine for pain.

And I did. A little of it.
But the best medicine had been that they had come to see
me.
That they had listened.
That I had seen concern in their faces.

The next day I was better,
and when they saw me they smiled,

and I remember them to this day.

Afterwards,
When I was out of the hospital and looked back
I said to myself that when the time came again
to be in a similar predicament,
I would ask of my friends
to take turns and be at my side,
if only for a few moments a day,
so that their presence,
their expressions and
their smiles,
would infuse me with the will to live
and to fight on.

Now, that's medicine for you.
Human contact.
Relating.
Connecting.

We need it.
We can't go on without it.
That is who we are.

So again,
say with me,
I am a man,
I will endure my pain
so I can understand and transform it,
for I have gifts in me that I must discover
and it takes a lifetime.

I am a man.

Look at your self as being made of different selves.
There's the kind self,
the assertive/aggressive self,
the hard working self,
the loving self
the defeatist self.

The assertive/aggressive self is very useful,
it's the self with initiative and drive,
and if in danger
will help get you out of trouble.
The other selves help you connect with fellow human beings
so you can make your way in the world
and create your space.

The defeatist self is of no help to you at all.
It's the aggressive self gone out of control,
the aggressive self turned destructive instead of constructive.

That's the mode you're in now,
defeating yourself and wanting to take others with you.

Stop it.

Let the other parts of you come in
and put a check on your defeatist self.

Do it.

Tell yourself
I will not surrender to my defeatist self.
Tell yourself,

I'm not in my right mind at this moment,
for if I were
I would not be stuck on the thought of giving up my life,
which is bad enough in itself,
but now I'm thinking of taking other people's lives,
as if they belonged to me,
as if I had a right to do so.

So please say,
I am angry and confused and I need help,
I need to reach out to someone
who can help me get over this very difficult moment,
for I want to be constructive instead of destructive.

Will someone please help me
hold my pain
so I won't hurt innocent people.

I am a man.

*D*on't like yourself?

Okay.

But you can work with it.
You can improve things.

One step at a time.

Don't know how to get to like yourself?
Let's get started:
Step one – acceptance.
Whatever you're feeling,
spill it out and spell it out.
Make a list.
On paper.
Put everything on it.
Don't leave anything out.

What did you just do?
Embraced honesty.
Saying I don't like what I'm feeling and owning it.

Feeling lonely?
Lover broke up with you?
Friends don't value you as you think they should?
Lost your job?
Feeling not appreciated at work?
Having trouble at school?
Don't think you're attractive?
Don't think you're smart?
Don't think you're tough?

Don't have any money?

Put it all down.

Feel a little silly?

Good.

We're on the right track.

Step two – blame everyone else.
Please start.

Parents, siblings, peers, friends, neighbors, acquaintances,
bosses, baristas, grocery clerks etc.

Feel better?

Not yet?
Okay. You haven't blamed enough people.
Keep trying.
Sooner or later you're going to run out of people to blame.
When you're done, turn the page.

•

*W*hen you've run out of people to blame, what's left?

You.

That's right.

Just you.

And that's what you need to get started on fixing your life.
Just you.

That's all we have, just ourselves.
To begin with.
But once we start reaching out,
then we have as much as we're willing to reach out for.

Yep.
There's kindness in this world.
Along with pain and misery and calamities and unfairness
and poverty and cruelty.
Along with all of it,
there's kindness in this world.

That's where you need to be now.

Asking for it.
Yes.
Asking for some kindness from the world.

And then what?

Once you receive it,
for you will receive it if you ask,
then you return the kindness.

But you have to ask first.
You have to climb over whatever pain or shame you now
have
that is choking you,
whatever pain or shame you feel crushed by
and ask for kindness from the world.

Once you receive it
then you return it.
How?
By making an effort.
An effort to improve your lot.

Step Three – accept yourself, whatever you're feeling. Same
as step one.

You need to go back to step one because you missed
something the first time around.

Breathe in and breathe out. Slowly.

Please say with me,
I am a man who's on the verge of hurting others
who have been through the same pain
I am now going through,

I am a man

in pain
Who's on the verge of hurting others
who have been through the same pain
I am now going through,
I am a man

And I want to be free.

That's right.

Say it,

I am a man
and I want to be free.

Repeat 100 times,

That's what you always have wanted,
the freedom to be all you can be.

If you want to pull the trigger and kill innocent people,
you are not a free man
but a slave to your pain,
instead of being its master.

Say it with me,

I will not be a slave to my pain

but its master.

Breathe in,

slowly,
breathe out,

I will not be a slave to my pain
but its master.

I am a man.

One day, some years ago, I was worried about something that was not going well.

While still trying to sort it out I went to buy some groceries at the nearby market.

My mind was still preoccupied when I turned into an aisle and looked up. I came to a sudden stop.

Right by the middle of the aisle, facing a shelf, a handicapped person was reaching up for an item.

The person was in a wheelchair and also had limited use of her arms and hands but she was still trying to get what she needed.

It was clearly hard for her but she was intensely focused on the task and gave no indication that she wanted help.

Walking in her direction I thought of offering my assistance but as I got close she finally grasped what she wanted and began to pull it off the shelf.

She smiled victoriously.

I walked past and felt lighter.

I wondered why and the answer came swiftly. My worries had left me.

Whatever it was that had concerned me was insignificant compared to the daily struggle that person had to endure.

Feeling trapped by your pain?

Look around.

Seek the gift of those who're worse off and endure.

They give it freely to anyone willing to pay attention.

Seek the gift of those who love life.

And you will find your own depth.

So what's life about?
Big question, but you might as well ask it,
for if you're about to pull the trigger and kill innocent people
then these moments you're living might be your last ones.

If we asked 100 people we would likely get 100 different
replies,
and the answer may vary depending on the season of life
you're living,
but let me offer you my idea.

Life is about being all you can be with what you have,
while you have it.
being all you can be with what nature gave you,
while it lasts.

Nature endowed you and me with possibilities,
possibilities that don't last a lifetime,
and it's up to you and me to make them happen,
while they're there.
It's up to each one of us to transform those potentials into
reality.

That's it.
That's the bottom line for me.
Of course, as I said,
it will be different for the next person.
I can only tell you what life means to me.

Life is not putting things off endlessly
but taking on risks every single day.
Small ones.

Large ones.
Risks to better your life.

Choice is critical.
We have various possibilities at any given time
and only so much energy to go around,
so we have to decide where to put our best efforts.

But whatever your choice,
Loving someone along the way is essential.
It doesn't have to be forever but it has got to happen at some
point.
Otherwise your full potential will not be realized.

This is basic to being human.
We need love to be all we can be.
We need to love someone so we can truly blossom.

It's one of the laws of nature.
I'm talking about loving with all you have.
Unrestrained.

You may have one love or many during your lifetime
but you've got to have at least one.
Your life is poor and unrealized if you can't say you loved.

You can love an idea, an occupation, doing something,
and that is essential to developing your potential,
but loving another human being is at the core.
You've got to put that in.

It's programmed into us.

It comes with our basic equipment.
And all we have to do is not get in the way of it and let it
flow.

Have you loved another human being?

If you haven't I'm here to tell you that you can.
And if you have done so and were not reciprocated
then I'm here to tell you that you will.

I know that.

There's someone out there for all of us.
Someone,
that if we show an interest in
will return our affections.

It may not be our first choice
or our second, third or tenth,
but I assure you that there's someone out there,
that if we show an interest in,
will return your affections.

Guaranteed.

If it hasn't happened to you
then you haven't let it happen,
which is part of the reason you're thinking
of pulling the trigger and killing innocent people.
Innocent people who have sought love and got it.
Or who are seeking it right now.

How much envy is there in your heart,
right this moment?

Be honest.

Breathe in and breathe out.
Acceptance.
Breathe in and breathe out.
Understanding.
Breathe in and breathe out.
Transformation.

As you think of pulling the trigger and killing innocent
people,
ask yourself,
how much envy is there in my heart?

I have not met you but I know,
that if you're thinking of killing innocent people
you have envy in your heart,
not just a little but a mountain of it,
a volcano of envy and rage that is about to explode
and scorch those around you,
because they appear to have what you don't have.

It's so sad.

Can't you feel that?
Please,
look into yourself,
can't you feel that?

Everyone out there who does not want to hurt another
person
is searching for their answers,
finding their depth,
like you should.

But out of envy and shame that you haven't put yourself out
and dared to live your life,
you now want to blame others for it,
and rip them of their possibilities.

Wow.

Does the thought not move you to tears?

Breathe.

But it doesn't have to be that way, does it?

So, please,
put the gun down and say,
I am a man.

Please.
I beg you,
say with me,
for the sake of your brothers and sisters,
for your own sake,
say with me,

I am a man with envy in my heart.

I am a man,
who could be doing better
but instead am choosing to give up,
to harm others,
to blame others
for my own failings
instead of facing them,
instead of staring my failings in the eye
and saying I accept you,
whatever you are,
I accept you and will bear my pain
and seek to understand it,
so I may transform it.

I am a man,
that in bearing my pain
will earn my freedom
for I will not be a slave to my pain
but the master of it,

I am a man.

●

*A*re you thinking of killing innocent people on
behalf of a cause or an idea?

Then you don't have a voice of your own
but are instead a pawn of the cause or idea.

So why not find your own voice instead?

Finding your own voice is becoming your own man.

Doesn't that sound attractive,
becoming your own man,
with your own opinions?

It takes thought. And enduring your pain. So you can
understand it and transform it.

Men with their own mind and their own voice,
men who have found their depth,
do not kill innocent people.

So breathe in and breathe out,
and say,

I am a man,
I have had murderous thoughts
but I will now relinquish them,
so I can set off on the journey
to find my own voice,
to find my own freedom.

I am a man.

Not a slave to my pain
but a master of it.

I am a man,
in search of my voice,
in search of my freedom.

I am a man.

•

$\mathscr{D}$on't think you have something to contribute?
Yes, you do.

Take the example of the person in the wheelchair who I ran
into in the market.
She did something for me
and she did it by living her life.

You don't know who you might be an inspiration for
but I assure you,
that as you set off on the journey to be all you can be
you will be an inspiration to others,
simply because you're willing to face your obstacles.

Every one of us has obstacles,
it doesn't matter how gifted you are,
you have obstacles.

Don't forget that we're all flawed.

And that you are unique.

There's no one like you on this earth.
No one.

So breathe in and breathe out,
say with me,
there's no one like me on this earth.

I belong.

I have a mind that I have to develop

and a voice I have to find,

I am a man in search of my freedom

I am a man.

$\mathcal{G}$uns

We need them to defend ourselves.
But we have to have limits.

At an international level we strive to arrange for arms
treaties,
mindful that the indiscriminate proliferation of weapons
is a waste of precious resources
and a threat to our existence.

The same should apply on a personal level.

Limits are essential so we can minimize the harm
should something go wrong,
should the person who was of perfectly sound mind
when he decided to amass a cache of weapons,
simply because he loved them,
then one day gets depressed and angry at the world,
or at the lover who walked out
or the employer that dismissed him
or whatever else.

We need to have limits because we humans are flawed.
We need to have limits on the number of weapons
anyone can possess at any given time
to minimize the damage they can cause.

It is sheer absurdity that we have not imposed limits
in the face of the lives we have lost
from the shootings of innocent people,
men and women, children, who did not get to live their lives,

who could have made enormous contributions to mankind,
to you and me.
And yet we allow this folly to continue.

Guns are used for sport. For hunting.
Okay.
You do not need an arsenal for that.
You do not because something could go very wrong.

You and I have to obey the speed limit, don't we?
Yes. Because something can go very wrong.
You and I can't drink to excess and then go driving, can we?
No. Because something will go very wrong.

We need limits when we live with others.

Living in the wild?
That's different.
You'll need your weapons to defend against threatening
wildlife
or to hunt and provide for yourself.

We need limits when we live with others.

Afraid government will become a tyrant and enslave you?
It could happen anywhere.
But how does the right to own all the guns you want deter
that from happening?

If government ever felt that it could enslave us
it would be because we failed to nurture public discourse
and the free exchange of ideas,

it would be because we failed to educate our people,
including the military,
because we failed to support our teachers,
it would be because we failed to keep our work force on the
cutting edge,

If government ever felt that it could enslave us
it would be because we allowed inequality to run rampant,
not because citizens had limits on the guns they could own.

Not having limits on the guns you can own is not what is
keeping our democracy alive,
and if you think that you're sadly deluded,
a delusion that the people of this country are paying
a heavy price for,
because those weapons that you're allowed to buy
are being turned against ourselves,
against our future.

You want to fight for our country?
Then fight to have your own voice,
and let the barrel of your gun be your developed mind,
and your bullets your creativity and thirst for knowledge.

Think of all the good we could do,
you and me both,
when we learn to value ourselves and others
no matter what the color of our skin, race or religion.

That's where the real fight is.

It is my fervent hope,

that one day soon we will look back on this time
and be baffled at how we allowed ourselves
to not impose limits on gun ownership,

And when we do we will grieve again
the loss of all those men, women and children
who died when we turned our guns against ourselves,
and we will grieve again
the loss of their contributions.

What will it take to open our eyes?

How many more lives?

How many more children?

*A*t any given moment
we're in various stages of development
and in various stages of disrepair.
All of us.
You and me.

But as pained as you may be
think of love and how it can heal,
and that love is in you, too.

I have not met you but I know that
there is love in you.

And if these words that I have written
with you in mind
make any sense,

Then share your pain

Please

And hope will spring forth.

So please,
reach out to someone,
a friend,
an acquaintance,
911.

Reach out to someone and ask for a little kindness.

We will all be grateful.

And you will too.

Oscar Valdes is the author of Letters to a Prisoner, Donald and Melania: 75 Days, US Korea Talks & Me Too, and the novel Walk Through Your Shadows. He lives and works in Los Angeles.